SUPERMAN

and the Villains on Venus

A SOLAR SYSTEM ADVENTURE

by Steve Korté
illustrated by Dario Brizuela

Superman created by Jerry Siegel and Joe Shuster
by special arrangement with the Jerry Siegel family

Consultant:
Steve Kortenkamp, PhD
Associate Professor of Practice
Lunar and Planetary Lab
University of Arizona
Tucson, Arizona

CAPSTONE PRESS
a capstone imprint

Clark Kent watches TV as he gets ready for work. Suddenly, a news bulletin breaks in. Professor Emil Hamilton from the world-famous S.T.A.R. Labs speaks to a reporter.

"Last night we detected a large spaceship heading toward Venus," Hamilton says.

Clark rips open his business suit. He is secretly Superman, the world's most powerful super hero.

"Up, up, and away!" says Superman, stepping outside and flying toward S.T.A.R. Labs.

At the lab, Professor Hamilton and Superman study an image of the spaceship on a video screen.

"This photo was taken by a space telescope orbiting Earth," says Hamilton.

Superman looks worried. "Could that ship really land on Venus?"

"It would need to be very durable to withstand the planet's high temperatures and pressure," says Hamilton.

"I recognize that spacecraft," says Superman. "It comes from an artificial satellite known as Warworld."

"I've never heard of it," says Hamilton with surprise.

Superman links Hamilton's computer to his own at the Fortress of Solitude. A dark world appears on the screen.

"This is Warworld," says Superman. "It's ruled by a monstrous villain called Mongul. He runs a gladiator pit where warriors fight battles to the death."

"What can you tell me about Venus?" asks Superman.

"It's the second planet from the Sun," says Hamilton, pulling up images on his screen. "And it's only five percent smaller in diameter than Earth."

"Are Venus and Earth similar?" asks Superman.

"Both planets are mostly made up of rock and metal," replies Hamilton. "Other than that, Venus is very different."

FACT

Venus has a thin crust, a rocky mantle, and a core made mostly of solid iron and some melted metals.

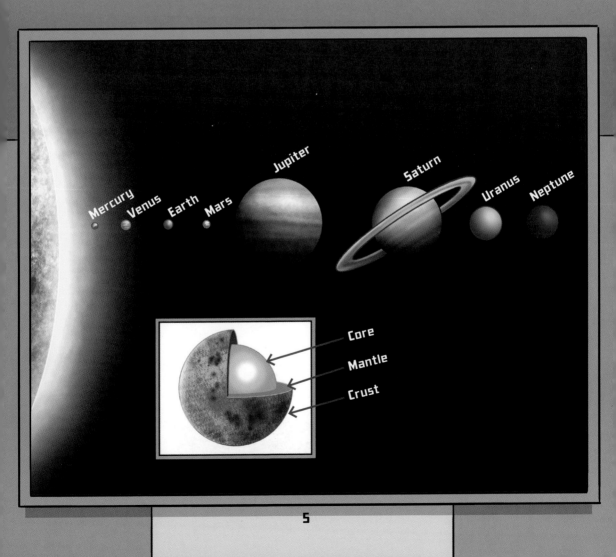

Mercury Venus Earth Mars Jupiter Saturn Uranus Neptune

Core

Mantle

Crust

"Billions of years ago, Venus may have had large oceans," says Hamilton. "But the planet's heat boiled the water away."

"Why is Venus so hot?" asks Superman.

"Its thick atmosphere is made mostly of carbon dioxide," says Hamilton. "This gas lets sunlight in to heat the planet, but then traps the heat inside."

"Just like sunlight passing through a greenhouse," says Superman.

"Exactly," replies Hamilton. "The greenhouse effect keeps Venus hot all day and night."

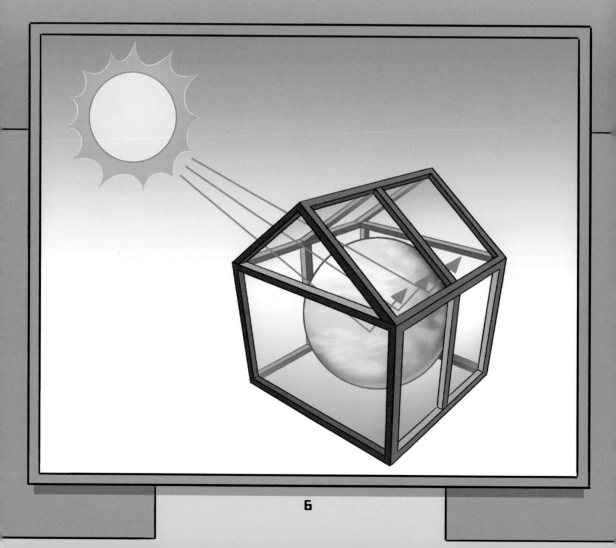

"Venus is also hot because thick clouds blanket the planet," says Hamilton, changing the image. "These clouds are made mostly of sulfuric acid."

"Sulfuric acid is poisonous to humans, right?" asks Superman.

"That's right," says Hamilton. "With acidic clouds and a carbon dioxide atmosphere, Venus would be a very unpleasant place to visit."

"I need to find out what Mongul is up to," says Superman. "How far is Venus from Earth?"

"That depends on the orbits of both planets," says Professor Hamilton. "Right now, Venus is very far at roughly 160 million miles, or 260 million kilometers, away."

"Then I'd better get going," says Superman. "I'll keep in touch using our radio transmitters."

Superman flies out a window
and soars into space. Soon, he
sees a bright planet streaked with
yellow and white.

"Does Venus have any
moons?" asks the Man of Steel.

"No," says Hamilton. "It's one
of two planets in our solar system
with no moons. Mercury is the
other planet."

"Professor, I'm flying through Venus' thick clouds," says Superman as he arrives at the planet. "I don't see a break in them anywhere."

"Those clouds block the Sun from shining on Venus, much like an overcast day on Earth," says Hamilton. "And Venus rotates clockwise, instead of counter-clockwise like Earth. If you could see the Sun rise on Venus, it would come up in the west and set in the east."

As Superman flies closer to Venus' reddish-brown surface, he feels something slowing him down.

"Wow, even I can feel the strong pressure here," says the Man of Steel.

"The weight of the planet's atmosphere pushes down with a pressure that is 90 times stronger than on Earth," says Hamilton. "It feels about the same as being nearly 3,000 feet, or 1 kilometer, under the ocean."

"Professor, I see Mongul's spaceship up ahead!" says Superman.

Superman lands on Venus. He spots the gladiator Draaga standing in front of the spaceship. The powerful warrior was taken from his planet and enslaved by Mongul years ago. Draaga is now the champion fighter on Warworld.

"Why are you here, Draaga?" asks Superman.

"Mongul wants to know if you are mighty enough to fight on Warworld," replies Draaga. "We will battle. Only one of us will leave this empty planet alive."

"And if I refuse?" asks Superman.

"Then Mongul will invade Earth," says Draaga with a growl.

"You don't have to do this, Draaga," says Superman. "Mongul had no right to make you a slave! If you will only—"

Before Superman can finish, Draaga growls and jumps forward.

WHAM!

Draaga's giant fist crashes against the Man of Steel's body. Superman tumbles to the ground.

Draaga grabs his giant axe and runs toward Superman. The axe's edge is made of Kryptonite, the only substance that can harm the Man of Steel.

"Prepare to meet your end, Superman!" yells Draaga, lifting the axe over his head.

Superman quickly rolls to one side.

CRASH!

The deadly weapon smashes into Venus' rocky surface.

The Man of Steel jumps to his feet and soars high above the ground.

"I want to wear out Draaga by forcing him to chase me, Professor," says Superman. "Tell me about the surface of Venus."

"We have a map of Venus' surface," says Hamilton. "We used radar waves to create it."

"Radar?" asks Superman with surprise. "Why not use unmanned spacecraft?"

"That hasn't been possible," says Hamilton. "The Russians landed 10 spacecraft on the planet between 1970 and 1984. But they only took pictures for about an hour before the planet's temperatures and pressure destroyed the spacecraft."

"But radar helped us see the planet's surface," continues Hamilton. "A spacecraft sent radar waves through the clouds and bounced them off Venus' surface. By measuring the time it took the waves to return to the spacecraft, we created images of the planet's landscape."

"The landscape below me reminds me of Earth," says Superman, swerving to avoid Draaga's axe.

"Yes, both planets have plains, mountains, and valleys," says Hamilton. "But volcanic lava covers more than 85 percent of Venus."

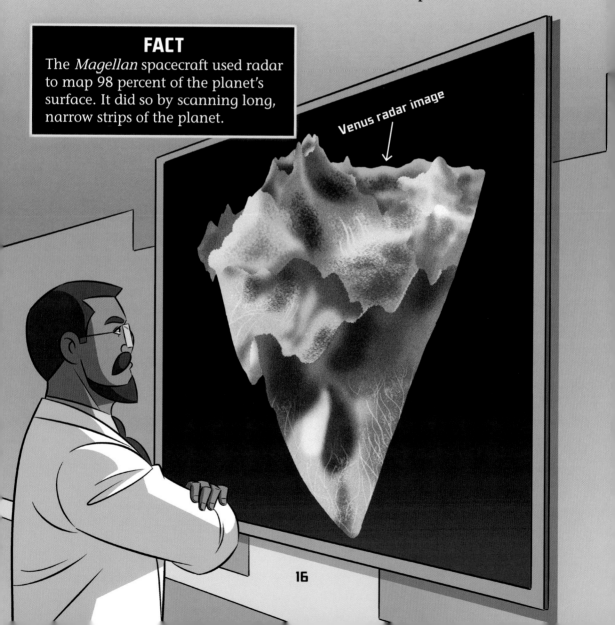

FACT
The *Magellan* spacecraft used radar to map 98 percent of the planet's surface. It did so by scanning long, narrow strips of the planet.

Venus radar image

"I see a large volcano up ahead," says Superman.

"Venus has more volcanoes than any other planet in the solar system," replies Hamilton. "It has more than 1,600 major volcanoes and hundreds of thousands of smaller ones."

"Are any of them still active?" asks Superman.

"We don't know," says Hamilton. "But we believe most of the lava covering Venus erupted 500 million years ago."

Suddenly, Draaga leaps in the air and grabs Superman's ankle. They both tumble to the planet's surface.

Draaga jumps to his feet and raises the Kryptonite axe.

ZAAAP!

The Man of Steel uses his heat-vision to shatter the axe's handle. Draaga yells in pain and drops the weapon.

Superman swings his legs around and trips Draaga. The villain tumbles into a giant hole.

"Draaga fell into a crater," says Superman.

"Venus has hundreds of asteroid impact craters," says Hamilton. "The smallest are about 4 miles, or 6 kilometers, wide. The largest are roughly 170 miles, or 270 kilometers, wide."

"This is one of the larger ones," says Superman, looking into the crater.

THUMP!

Draaga's massive hand grasps the crater's edge. Then the villain clamps his other hand onto Superman's wrist.

Superman leaps into the air with Draaga in tow. The Man of Steel does a dozen quick somersaults. Draaga grows dizzy and releases his grip.

THUD!

Draaga crashes to the ground. Seconds later, he chases Superman once again.

"Professor, I'm flying toward Venus' north pole," says Superman. "I see a giant mountain range ahead."

"That's Maxwell Montes, the largest mountain range on Venus," says Hamilton.

"Professor, is that snow on the mountaintops?" asks Superman.

"No," replies Hamilton. "It's likely melted metal. Venus' surface is so hot that minerals on the ground vaporize and rise into the atmosphere. The metals then cool, freeze, and fall onto the mountaintops like shiny, metallic snowflakes."

"This ends here!" shouts Draaga, leaping up and wrapping his arms around Superman's chest.

CRASH!

They both fall onto the side of the mountain.

FACT

Maxwell Montes is named after James Clerk Maxwell. His work with radio waves allowed scientists to use radar to map the surface of Venus.

Draaga squeezes Superman tighter and tighter.

The Man of Steel uses his super-strength to expand his chest and flex his arms. Superman breaks Draaga's grip and spins around.

"This *does* end here!" declares Superman.

WHOOOSH!

A blast of powerful super-breath pours from Superman's mouth. The villain tumbles down the side of Maxwell Montes.

The Man of Steel flies down and stands over Draaga at the base of the mountain. The villain glares at Superman.

"You are the champion," says Draaga. "I am prepared to die."

Superman shakes his head. "I will not take your life, Draaga."

An astonished look fills Draaga's face. "But death is the fate of all fallen gladiators on Warworld!"

Hours later, Draaga approaches Mongul's spaceship. He carries Superman over his shoulder.

Mongul opens the spaceship's hatch. He smiles as Draaga approaches.

"I see you defeated Earth's so-called champion," says Mongul. "Bring him into the ship. We will bury him on Warworld."

"Draaga, set a course for Warworld," commands Mongul, smiling at the fallen hero on the floor of his ship.

"No," replies Draaga.

Mongul spins around in anger. "You dare to defy your master?" he shouts, raising his arm to strike Draaga.

ZAAAP!

Superman jumps to his feet and blasts Mongul with his heat-vision. Then Draaga delivers a mighty blow to Mongul's chest. The villain crumples to the floor, unconscious.

Soon, the Man of Steel carries Mongul through Venus' clouds and out into space.

"Is everything all right, Superman?" asks Hamilton.

"Just fine," Superman replies. "But I'll need your help to build the strongest prison cell on Earth to serve as Mongul's new home."

"What about Draaga?" asks Hamilton.

The Man of Steel smiles as Mongul's spaceship zooms up behind him.

"Draaga is heading home as well," says Superman.

- Venus has had several names through time. The ancient Babylonians named it Ishtar, after the daughter of their moon god. The Greeks thought it was two stars and named them Phosphorus and Hesperus. When they realized it was a planet, they named it Aphrodite, after their goddess of love. The Romans later named it after their own goddess of love, Venus.

- Venus is the only planet named after a female. All but one of Venus' surface features are also named after women. That includes the planet's plains, craters, and volcanoes.

- The Italian astronomer Galileo Galilei used a telescope in 1610 to learn that Venus had phases like the Moon. His study of Venus helped prove that the Sun was the center of the solar system. Before then, many people believed that the other planets orbited Earth.

- Venus is the easiest planet to see from Earth. It is sometimes called the "morning star" or "evening star" because it can be seen just before sunrise or just after sunset.

- A day on Venus is very long. It takes 117 Earth days for Venus to spin around once. It takes the planet 225 Earth days to journey around the Sun.

- Venus has three large highland areas: Aphrodite Terra, Ishtar Terra, and Lada Terra. If Venus had oceans, these highland areas would be continents.

- In 1962, NASA's unmanned *Mariner 2* flew by Venus. It was the first time a planet was visited by a spacecraft.

- In 1970, Russia's *Venera 7* became the first spacecraft to successfully land on the surface of Venus. It was also the first craft ever to send back data from the surface of another planet.

- The last spacecraft to land on Venus was *Vega 2* in 1985. NASA and Russia's space program may work together to send a lander to the planet in 2025.

GLOSSARY

asteroid (AS-tuh-royd)—a large space rock that moves around the Sun; asteroids are too small to be called planets

astronomer (uh-STRAH-nuh-muhr)—a scientist who studies stars, planets, and other objects in space

atmosphere (AT-muhss-fihr)—the layer of gases that surrounds some planets, dwarf planets, and moons

carbon dioxide (KAHR-buhn dy-AHK-syd)—a colorless, odorless gas

core (KOR)—the inner part of a planet or moon that is made of metal or rock

crater (KRAY-tuhr)—a hole made when asteroids and comets crash into a planet or moon's surface

gladiator (GLAD-ee-ay-tur)—a warrior who fights other warriors or animals in order to entertain people

lava (LAH-vuh)—the hot, liquid rock that pours out of a volcano when it erupts

orbit (OR-bit)—the path an object follows as it goes around the Sun or a planet

satellite (SAT-l-ahyt)—an object that moves around a planet or other cosmic body

solar system (SOH-lur SISS-tuhm)—the Sun and the objects that move around it

READ MORE

Beckett, Leslie. *Exploring Venus.* Journey Through Our Solar System. New York: KidHaven Publishing, 2018.

Black, Vanessa. *Venus.* Space Voyager. Minneapolis: Bullfrog Books, 2018.

Carlson-Berne, Emma. *The Secrets of Venus.* Smithsonian Planets. North Mankato, Minn.: Capstone Press, 2016.

TITLES IN THIS SET

SUPERMAN AND THE MENACE ON MERCURY

A SOLAR SYSTEM ADVENTURE

SUPERMAN and the Villains on Venus

A SOLAR SYSTEM ADVENTURE

SUPERMAN AND THE INVASION OF EARTH

A SOLAR SYSTEM ADVENTURE

SUPERMAN and the Mischief on Mars

A SOLAR SYSTEM ADVENTURE

INDEX

INTERNET SITES

Use FactHound to find Internet sites related to this book.
Visit *www.facthound.com*
Just type in 9781543515664 and go.

Published by Capstone Press in 2018
1710 Roe Crest Drive
North Mankato, Minnesota 56003
www.mycapstone.com

Cataloging-in-publication information is on file with the Library of Congress.
ISBN 978-1-5435-1566-4 (library binding)
ISBN 978-1-5435-1577-0 (paperback)
ISBN 978-1-5435-1585-5 (eBook PDF)

Editorial Credits
Christopher Harbo, editor; Kayla Rossow, designer; Laura Manthe, production specialist

Summary: Superman squares off against the super-villains Draaga and Mongul in an
adventure that reveals the remarkable features and characteristics of the planet Venus.

Illustration Credits
Gregg Schigiel (Superman): back cover, 1, 32

Printed in the United States of America.
PA017